Depression in verses

Depression is an unseen beast

For anyone who feels these words the way I felt them when I wrote them, always remember you are not alone.
You don't need to fight alone.
You don't need to struggle alone.
Depression is an unseen beast and fighting it alone will cause more damage than good.

It began here

I am a 35 year old man and I've had an ongoing battle with mental health most of my life. I discovered poetry whilst struggling with my mental health. It became my outlet, my form of relief.

It would only be natural for me to release my first book from my new pamphlet collection "In Verses" about depression.

This book holds a collection of poems and verses written while I was struggling with depression. Some of what you will read may be upsetting, it may be a trigger or it may simply open your eyes into the world of mental health as you have never seen it before. It may make you feel less alone.

Depression is a hard fight and hard to live with but I find peace in words.

Contents

Don't let a smile fool you

Don't let that smile fool you,
The face doesn't hold the pain in you,
Pent up stress,
A world of depressed,
A smile will make another day like the rest.

A grin doesn't make it ok,
A smirk didn't take the battles away,
That daily fight,
The dark thoughts at night,
Damaged but a smile hides a broken life .

A giggle doesn't mean what it's meant too,
A chuckle hides the hurt inside you,
Fake laughter becomes a trick,
Why would someone want to see the sick?
Holding a false front becomes a way to disguise it.

Robert Gillett

A broken mind

A broken mind is a dangerous place,
Not visible through the smile on a face.

Some days

Some days I'm at peace,
I'm happy,
Proud of my life and my daily achievements whilst living in a
persistent fight.

Other days I'm broken,
Destroying myself,
Chipping away at the pieces of the positive I have left leaving
only a wreck.

I struggle with the truth of which is the real me.
Stuck between the peace and the broken,
Am I happy in the destruction?

I'm lost in myself,
Is this who I am or is it just bad Mental health?

Internal phantom

An internal phantom,
A demon hidden in the physiological pathways,
Picking at the weak brain waves,
Breaking the mental state.
Taking you prisoner in your own body,
Reflection looking eerily dissimilar,
This feeling is so familiar.

Why can't I cry

Why can't I cry?
I'm lost,
It's bad luck,
Loss in body trust,
It keeps giving up,
My mental health can't keep up,
I'm digging out of hell but I can't reach to the top,
The end light keeps drifting or am i still sinking,
I have no hope left,
My sanity goes right but im passing left,
Suicide or breakfast what a fucking thought process,
I'm not sure how much fight I have left.
I'm lost.
When I feel myself falling away I need catching but I'm too
proud to shout so I fall in silence,
Though the tough days and the tense days I keep it hidden
and it stays,
I stay in pain,
Too many emotions locked away in my brain,
Why ain't I shouting,
Why can't I cry,
I'm left lost contemplating different ways to die.

Robert Gillett

Why can't I cry,

I need help but I can't ask,

I'm not allowed to ask,

I'm a man bury this shit deep,

My emotions shouldn't be weak so I continue to mask.

I'm my own worst enemy but I'm the only one inside my

head that knows what's going on with me,

I'm crashing in there,

I feel I'm going crazy but i shut the door behind as I walked

into the self sabotage and no one can understand me.

I look so calm and I'm face filled with smiles,

So no one knows,

No one understands,

Why can't I let them know?

Why can't I cry?

One shot

Those days I can't take anymore,
I'm lost fighting the man inside my head that's internally
destroying me,
He's telling me I'd be better off dead,
Even at my best it's not good enough,
This mental health fucking destroys me.
I get to tired of fighting,
I feel like I'm losing,
It's frightening.
There's days I can't take it,
I wanna just give up,
What if I just stopped
Put a gun to my head,
Pulled the trigger,
One shot.

Robert Gillett

I hate that day

I hate that day,
That day when something hurts in a different type of way,
Head is crushing with a new type of ache.

Depression comes from nowhere and decides to bite,
Anxiety pops up and causes that inner fight,
You've had twisting thoughts keeping you awake all night.

Body is fine but it feels a broken state,
Skin is on fire with no signs of flames,
Waking up in a wreck and there's nothing to blame.

These sudden symptoms simply interrupt,
Another day without reason your body has gone corrupt,
I hate that day,
It's that day I wish I could give up.

You see a smile

You don't see what's behind the eyes,
You don't see the pain inside someone's mind.
You don't see the thoughts keeping people awake at night,
You see a smile.

You don't the struggle happening beneath,
You don't see someone's personal grief,
The don't see the losses snatched away by an invisible thief,
You see a smile.

You don't see the strength it takes,
You don't see the internal battle that's holding off the
downward brake,
You don't see the fear when someone eventually loses faith,
You see a smile.

You don't see someone knock down that negative wall,
You didn't see them fighting trying to overcome it all,
You don't see the little win for courage so they can stand tall,
You see a smile.

Robert Gillett

You don't see the gratitude for that one good day,
You don't see the happy that finally came with a small mental change,
You don't see the joyous moment when depression eventually gives way,
You see a smile.

What happened to you?

What happened to you?
You're changing,
You're not that same person anymore,
I'm watching you fade,
You're slowly disappearing.

What's happening to you?
You were the coolest guy in the room,
So confident,
Always up for a laugh,
Never afraid to crack that cheeky smile.

What happened to you?
You were a legend.
Then you started to change.
You're always depressed,
Anxious,
You're a blatant wreck.
I miss that guy you were before.

Robert Gillett

I hate watching this happen to you.
Let me help you fix this,
Let me help you find your way back,
I miss you,
I just want to help you.

I can't stand by and watch this happen to you.
The disease didn't change you,
It's just twisting the insides of your head,
This mess in your headspace is what's left when MS and
depression decide to collide,
That legend you are?
He's just hiding inside.

Inspiration

People call me an inspiration,
I struggle with that,
People thank me for what I do,
I struggle with that too.

I suffer with depression,
I'm fighting demons in my head,
I wake stressed most days,
Wondering if I would be better off dead.

I live with a disability,
One that's killing me but won't take my life,
An illness that's crippling me,
Taking pieces one day at a time.

So I write,
I write my words to keep me alive,
I write my words to express my pain,
I continue to write,
It's what gets me through most days.

Robert Gillett

How can I be an inspiration?
I'm always suffering,
How can people be proud?
I haven't done anything.

My career grows,
I even wrote a book,
I struggle with the success,
I can't stop thinking about what this disease has took.

Robbie, what's wrong with you?
Look at everything you're achieving!
I know,
It's just hard,
I can't help what I've been thinking.

Behind the words there is still a broken man,
Behind the words I'm still suffering,
I can't be an inspiration,
I haven't done anything.

Braving waters

I get sick of braving the waters,
I get tired of being strong,
I just want to hide in my head,
That's where I feel I belong.

I want to fall deep in the rabbit hole,
Stay there and hide,
Keep anxiety and depression from eating my mind.

Mental thoughts in my scarred depressive brain,
Keep changing my course,
Literally turning me insane.

I wish life was simple,
My thoughts would give me less,
I can't be bothered with life,
When my heads a fucking mess.

Robert Gillett

That smile

How many times has my smile been a lie?
Can people not see it when they look me in the eye?
I've become too good at hiding my pain,
Become too good at not being seen,
Not on purpose,
People just think I'm being me.

Surface level people think I'm great,
People call me a fighter,
What they don't know is I'm barely a survivor.

My illness crushes me,
Depression sits forefront and snatches away my positivity,
Anxiety just watches,
It waits,
For that right moment just to shock me into panic
destroying my mental state.

That smile I'm holding,
That smile,
Is it real?
Maybe.........

You're depressed

Robbie, you're depressed!

No im not,
How can you even say that?
I'm smiling,
Cracking jokes,
Always being silly,
Can you not see that?

Honestly Robbie I think you are.

Seriously I'm not ,
I think you're obsessed,
Calling me depressed,
Look at me and the way that I'm dressed,
My behaviour is at its best,
I'm sunny inside and I feel genuinely blessed,
What on earth makes you think I'm depressed?

Robbie, take a long look at yourself.

Why are you not taking me seriously?
I'm not sad,

I'm hardly ever mad,
I look at my life and I'm really glad!
I'm actually proud of what I have!
So why are you saying this about me?

Look Robbie you can't lie to me,
I'm that little man in your head,
The one who sees you crying in bed,
Wondering if you can actually live up to what you've just
said,
How many times can you think that it would be easier if you
were dead?
Don't think I don't notice these things

Stop lying to yourself,
Depression is a hard fight,
Please can we get some help?

Mental health

In life no one is supposed to struggle,
Mental health is not supposed to be an issue,
So why when someone that struggles with mental health
does it make life an issue?
An issue for somebody else?
An issue for someone not struggling,
An issue for someone looking from the outside that has no
idea what someone is dealing with on the inside.

Why is it a problem for them?
Why are we not allowed to talk?
Why are we ridiculed for suffering?
Why do we live in a society where we are punished for it?

Talking is an escape,
Talking can set you free,
Talking can get you support and help you be where you
need to be.
So why the fuck are we punished?

Why would you call someone names for being depressed?
Why would you kick someone when they're down?
Kick them when they are broken?

Robert Gillett

This judgemental world is full of bullies and trolls,
Inconsiderate people,
People hurting people,
Taking pieces of their souls.

First hand I've seen this,
First hand I've suffered with it,
I've been been emotionally battered from the people that are
supposed to care the most,
It only makes things worse,
Where are you then supposed to turn when fighting a
depressive curse?

Why does no one want to listen!
What are you supposed to do?
Should you internalise your pain,
Hideaway inside your head?
There is no wonder so many depressed people end up dead,
At funerals people are saying I wish I could have done more,
These same people helped the decline 6 ft below the floor.
Where is the support?

Man in the mirror

That man in the mirror hates me,
I see him smiling,
Why's he smiling at me?
He's laughing and joking,
But I'm a wreck,
I'm in pain,
My skins on fire,
And that man is laughing.

I live in and out of bouts of depression but this guy in the
mirror wants to crack jokes at me,
I see him telling me it's all okay,
You'll get through another hard day,
I'm crumbling inside but he wants to pat me on the back
with small talk.

I'm sure he hates me,
He's always lies,
He looks so good,
Cap on,
Tracksuit,
He looks fresh,
He makes me feel disgusting,

How can he go on like that?

No one understands what's on the other side of the mirror,

Seeing is believing?

Well that guy looks good,

He's happy,

Such a joker,

He's so good at putting on front,

I hate that guy in the mirror,

He's a lying fucking cunt!

Nothing helps

There's a light in me somewhere,
I reach for it,
But i struggle to find it,
To see it,
It's gone.

The beautiful soul I have,
It hides,
Keeping itself hidden in the darkness where I feel I belong.

The real smile that I should have is covered by a mask of a
thousand lies.

The future people say I deserve is dying as each minute
passes by.

I'm lost,
I'm losing myself,
Nothing helps.

Robert Gillett

Positivity

Living a life being ill all the time takes its toll on you,
It's consuming,
Constantly hard work.

Trying to keep your thought process positive whilst fighting
a persistent ever changing disability is too hard.

I struggle with the change in me,
Struggle with the challenge my life has become,
Some days I'm positive,
"I got this"
Others I'm in absolute distress,
I still try my best,
Some days I don't want to continue,
Others,
Honestly I don't want to tell you.

I hate being ill,
I hate what it's done to me,
I live for better days and try to grasp some positivity.

Thoughts in my head

I hate this mental health,
These thoughts in my head,
How can I wake up one morning wishing I was dead?
I was alright yesterday,
Happy,
Joking,
I had A good day.

So what the fuck happened?
How can negative thoughts and rough sleep cause this crazy
decline in me?

I can't cope feeling this way,
It's messing with my brain,
I went from doing well to driving myself insane.

Robert Gillett

Need a friend

How can I turn myself into a friend instead of staring in the
mirror and seeing the enemy,
That guy looking back at me will surely be the end of me.

Keep going

When I'm struggling to cope,
When I'm losing hope,
When I feel broken with no where to go,
I keep going,

When I'm too tired to move,
When wins feel like a lose,
When I'm fighting the path I didn't choose,
I keep going,

When people stop and just stare,
When I watch them lose care,
When I'm struggling and I'm feeling that life isn't fair,
I keep going.

Beyond the eye

Beyond the eye there is more than you could imagine.
If seeing wasn't all that mattered life would be unbelievably
different.

Best friend

You were my Best Friend,
You was always there,
You are the one who I trust,
You are the one that cares.

So why are you attacking me?
You've done this before,
This time it's too bad,
I can't take it anymore!

You're picking at my faults,
You're even calling me names!
I'm done with you,
I'm done with your stupid games.

Why won't you leave?
I just can't get away,
I'm sick of you beating on me,
It's every single day.

I fight you,
But you're stronger,
I hide,

Then you find me,
I'd deceive you,
But you're smarter,
I can't escape you,
I need to be free.

How has it come to this?
You're supposed to be my friend.
How is it that death is the only way this will end?

You want to end it,
But I don't want to die.
All I can do is plead,
I keep asking myself why.

As I see you in the mirror,
I tell you I don't want to play your game!
Why do we keep fighting?
We are both one,
We are both the same.

How to fix a broken man

How to fix a broken man?
Talk?
Speak out?
That doesn't work.
Kill your self?
Run away?
These won't help,
Get Peace n quiet?
Now you're stuck with your thoughts.

How do you fix yourself?
Think of your kids?
Think of your wife?
Think for yourself?
I can't do this.
I'm broken.
Thinking doesn't help!

Call the helpline!
It's engaged?
Now what?
Listen to music?
Just makes you worse,

Robert Gillett

Think of past times?
That's what got you here in the first place!

Now what?
Pull your socks up?
Get over it?
Bottle it up?
Have a drink?
Take some drugs?
Crack a joke?
Bury it so deep no one can find it.

Why are you broken?
You have it all?
Great kids,
Wonderful wife,
How can I be broken?
I have an amazing life.

Refuse to lose

I refuse to lose,
This saying in life I've become a custom to,
Diagnosed with a disability,
Battling mental health has become a daily routine,
I refuse to lose,
It doesn't matter how many times I crash,
I still refuse.
The challenges I face daily have become harder,
The illness that I have progresses so I must fight harder.
I need to pick myself up time and time again,
Each time becomes more difficult but still I refuse to lose.

If losing was an option it would be easy,
If quitting was a possibility, who would I be?
Would I stay hidden?
Lose myself to an endless whirlwind of depression?
Show the world around me to just hide away and give up?

Despite the difficulties I live with I can't do that,
I must be strong,
Show my children to be strong,
Show the world around me we all have the strength inside us
and we all have the power to overcome.

Robert Gillett

I'll get through everything that will be delivered to me,

Of course I'll get knocked along the way,

I've already survived everything I've faced all the way up to this day.

I have been beaten but I've never lost,

I come back every time no matter the damage or the physiological cost.

You are you

Anxiety,
Depression,
Disability,
Don't let them win and keep you from being you,
Don't be defined by the destructive illnesses that
consistently take from you,
They are not you.
You are you.

Possession

You get lost,
Sucked into the world of anxiety and depression,
For this there's no lesson,
There's no release,
It keeps you,
It won't release you,
Forever it holds you in its possession.

Dark night

That dark night falls in,
Windows are closed with the drapes drawn,
Doors bolted,
Heating alight to protect against bitter ice setting in.
Familiar faces,
Their loving embraces,
Not a more treasured place,
A crowd in the abode,
So why do you feel alone?

House is filled with light and personality,
It's still dark out of your eyes,
A dimmer switch only for you.
Voices are in a peaceful motion,
Yet you feel commotion,
Isolated condemnation,
Emotions are broken.

Tearful yet tearless,
Tears should be running down the face like the rain crashing
against the window pain,
Instead the face runs dry,

Robert Gillett

Nor a resemblance of a broken cry,
Passing thoughts for that disappearing twinkle that used to
fill the eye.

Your soft temperament and nice nature,
Replaced with the anger of an ogre,
Invisible to see,
Fraudulent joy sits on your posture,
A half witted smile the face holds,
A forever unruly fronting of an internal mans worn,
The depression's surface is peaceful but the inside is
distorted and torn.

The dark night falls in,
Windows are closed with the drapes drawn.

I'm still standing

The complexities of this life can be too difficult to live with,
Always fighting yourself in my own head,
You find yourself worthless,
Useless,
There's a complete barrier to the way you feel and what is
reality.
I get lost in my own head fighting those thoughts,
Always fighting those demons,
They consistently take the life from me,
Take the light from me,
There's no difference to the way I behave from winning days
to losing days.
No difference to you but me it's two completely different
worlds,
Smiles, joy and optimism,
Or anger, frustration and pessimism.
It's like having Dr Jekyll and Mr Hyde battle for control in
my mind but I'm only hurting myself, inside,
But I'm still standing.

Robert Gillett

I hide myself away,

Wish my days away,

I wish my bad days would leave and give me a break,

For my heads sake,

My family's sake,

I'm not sure how much of this one person is supposed to take,

But I continue to take it,

I'm my own punching bag and I don't hold back the punches.

I've taken too many physiological beatings from the person who should love me the most.

I try positive reinforcement to keep myself upright,

masking myself with smiles and laughter so no one can see to struggle,

I don't know how I do it but I keep going,

I know why I do it so I keep going,

I am strong inside and I survive every beating I deliver myself,

Refusing to be beaten by mind breaking mental health,

I fight and I keep fighting.

I fight persistently to avoid another suicidal crash landing,

But for now,

I'm still standing.

Trigger

If I had a trigger to pull,
Would I have pulled it?
Put the pistol to my head and ended my days,
I've been in to many positions where I don't see another way,
But I know I'll see you there,
You're that angel at the handle telling me no,
Telling me this ain't the way to go,
There's a better way to release it all,
Life doesn't need to end with your brains splattered against
the wall.

Inside

I get lost,
I face the pain caused by my brain,
Sucking the soul from the inside of me, I need saving,
Somebody save me,
I feel im dying inside,
I have these pains that no one can see,
This destruction is hidden within me,
Heart of a warrior with the body of a leper, Damaged,
I'm hiding the cost of internal demolition,
Falling back,
Sinking back,
Crying inside.

Within

I'm always trying my best,
Happy one day,
The rest?
I'm sick,
I'm depressed.

Sometimes I'm on top of the world,
I love life,
Feel like I'm flying.
Others I want to hideaway,
Feel like I'm dying.

Living like this is hard,
I hope it will one day be easy,
People give me their kindness,
Hoping it will relieve me,

It works for a moment,
Then I end up back where I started,
Sad,
In pain,
Usually broken hearted!

Robert Gillett

Even with the support around me,
All their comforting words,
Doctors, my family and friends,
No one can fix the hurt.

I do what I can to move forward,
Not let this disease win,
Show everyone a smile,
Not the hurt within.

Drama queen

You call me a drama queen?
There's no drama in depression,
I need your help and not for you to insult me,
I need your support not your name calling,
The more you behave like this the more I feel myself
falling......

Robert Gillett

The beast

I can't see the beast I fight,
I just know that it's there,
It's always with me,
I carry it with me everywhere.
You can't see this horrid beast,
Its not visible to the eye,
This beast lives within me,
In my body and in my mind,
It tries to take parts of me slowly,
I wrestle with it day and night,
It's a unpredictable beast,
It attacks me unknowingly,
It does it whenever it likes.
I will never stop fighting the beast,
I promise I will never give in,
I will fight this beast all the way to the grave,
One day I will die,
Or just maybe,
One day I'll win.

You've got this

You've got this mate,
You're a fighter,
You know it,
You've got this.

Keep positive,
Stay smiling,
Stay strong,
You've got this.

Absorb the pain,
Stand straight,
Chin up,
You've got this.

Taking a turn,
Emotionally breaking,
Losing my grip,
Have you still got this?

Robert Gillett

Dying inside,
You're falling away,
Can't take any more,
I don't know if I've got this..........

Believe

I must keep going,
Must keep Fighting,
Surviving,
Believing.

Robert Gillett

Don't lose yourself

Don't lose yourself in a fight you haven't lost,
You can survive a fight without "yourself" being the cost.

Your scars make you who you are.

Emotional scars remind you of a time that was hard,
Cracked pieces in the mentality of who you are,
Memories you'd wish could be forgotten but they harbour a
past of what made you at the present.

Surface scars like the cuts in your arm or the gash from your
face,
Take you back to a place reminding you of the mistakes,
A closed wound visible serving as an inclination of who you
were and to show you the battles you have fought.

Robert Gillett

Fear

Fear of the inner thoughts,
Dangerous thinking,
Internal taunts.

Fear of the perception,
The wrong judgement,
A misunderstood reflection.

Fear of the unknown,
The unkindly perspective,
The horror of alone.

The fear of the surrender,
The undesirable end,
The dead only remembered.

That doesn't help

Not seeing isn't the same as ignoring,
Not understanding isn't the same as refusal to listen,
Supporting someone isn't moaning behind them,
Lifting someone isn't putting them down.

Hoping for the best doesn't come after a negative breath,
Wanting to help shouldn't be a negotiation,
Lending a hand isn't taking with the other,
Being somewhere to assist isn't demanding a gift.

Support comes from love and honesty,
A lift might be an open eye,
Help comes from the ones who care,
Changing someone's world can be just wanting to be there.

Robert Gillett

Take one step

Take one step,
Just one step forward,
And breath.
One step away from the past,
One step away from the damage,
That mental carnage that now sits one step behind you.
Don't look back,
Don't look back at the stack of troubles you are now one
step away from.
The first step was hard and hold that in regard as you
embrace your pace and take one more step.
One more step of release and relief as you begin to distance
yourself from your former self.
Keep the steps moving,
One,
Then two,
A new path you have made for you.
A fresh world of belief.
It can be here,
In front of you,
If you could just believe.

Heal

A broken man is not who you are,
You have wounds that need to heal.
Damaged but not beyond repair,
You are still in there.

The mirror lies

What can see you staring at you when you look in the
mirror?
You and your reflection are the same,
The person on the other side doesn't change,
It's the same,
It's the same in image but not in mental regard which makes
it hard.

People say you look great,
How you tell them they're wrong because you've seen this
image?
That cause of confusion belongs in your head not in the eyes
of someone else.
You explain the pain and the mental distress which an
onlooker can't process because you look fine.
The mirror says you are lying.

The perplexed reflection of how you feel and the picture
you're holding are too different,
Two worlds apart,
The suffering you hold in your heart and that feeling of
being broken apart are dismissed,
Misunderstood because the mirror disguised the truth.

Putting on a front

I became too good at putting on a front,
Sometimes I'm not actually sure if it's a front or not,
I leave myself questions,
Am I happy today or am I lying to myself?
Yesterday I was needing help.

The front I hold is happy whether Im happy or not,
Whether I'm anxious or not,
Depressed or not.
I've become too good at visually lying to everyone,
How is anyone supposed to help me if I don't let them see?
What would it matter anyway?
No one really wants to help a depressive me.....

Robert Gillett

Seek

When the darkness sets,
Seek the light.

When the clouds form over,
Seek shelter.

When the walls cave in,
Seek support.

When you reach the bottom,
Seek the way up.

When the path becomes impossible,
Seek a new route.

When you feel defeated,
Seek the fight in you.

Sometimes I wanna get real fucked up. v1

Sometimes I wanna get real fucked up.
I feel I wanna smoke so much weed I become one with the
trees and I get wavey.

I could float away on a pillow of soft clouds and daze my
way through the day,
Then drift into mindfulness space,
I could just peacefully lay.

I would be at one with the earth,
Discover my spiritual worth,
Conquer the world in my magical dreams,
Find my inner truth hiding amongst the trees.

Wake up in the woods with twigs sticking out of my hair
and no idea how I got there....

Robert Gillett

Sometimes I wanna get real fucked up. v2

Sometimes I wanna get real fucked up.
I wanna get so drunk at the end of the night I fall asleep
hugging a strangers toilet.

I could gatecrash someone's party,
Air guitar to the ace of spades,
Stroke some random guys moustache that's hanging off his
face.

Buy everyone a drink because I think I'm made of bloody
money,
Eat a fatty kebab and dribble the sauce all over me.

Wake up the next day covered in spew,
People are embarrassing me when I ask them what the fuck
did I do....

Sometimes I wanna get real fucked up. v3

Sometimes I wanna get real fucked up.
I wanna get on the cocaine,
Rushing so much I could beat forest gump in an endurance
race.

I'd be that guy at the bar chatting shit about anything,
I'd think I'd know everything,
A few lines of Charlie and I've become the knowledge king,
I'd feel so hard I could knock out Tyson fury the gypsy king.

I could rave,
Party all night until most people are getting out of bed,
Using dumb lines like don't worry I'll rest when I'm dead.

But reality,
I've spent most of my night in the corner, dripping with
sweat, talking nonsense and chewing his face off.
I'd wake up in the morning with all my money gone....

Robert Gillett

Sometimes I wanna get real fucked up. v4

Sometimes I wanna get real fucked up.
I wanna take magic mushrooms,
Break into an abandoned house and just trip.

Sit there alone in apprehension waiting for that psychedelic
kick,
Sweating so much I get down to pants,
Rolling around the carpet escaping imaginary purple ants,
Get up and do a crazy zulu dance in silence.

Fight an invisible Teddy bear,
Ripping out the monsters that are attached to my hair that
are not even there.

Then get arrested because the abandoned house was actually
the neighbours....

Sometimes I wanna get real fucked up. v5

Sometimes I wanna get real fucked up,
Mental health makes me wanna get real fucked up.

I remind myself that getting fucked up would only be
running away,
It would only be an escape,
I need to keep myself safe.

I can't float away in a breeze,
I can do the air guitar sober,
I don't need to knock out a boxer,
Or dance around in my pants.

I need to tell myself that it's ok,
I made it though one more day.

Sometimes I wanna get real fucked up,
But I won't....

Robert Gillett

Don't let depression be the end of you.....

A little message

Depression is real and it's so hard to live with. The ups and downs in life can sometimes be too much to handle. The happy one minute and broken the next is consuming and confusing but yet we carry on.
If you are struggling please find a place to reach out. Sometimes this is easier said than done and I completely understand that. People inside your inner circle may also be a bad place to look for support sometimes but there is support out there, I promise you. There are many places of support you may be yet to discover.

My escape is words and verses.
If you're struggling please find yours.

Much love

Robbie
Beneath The Tracksuit

Special thanks

Depression is evil and living with it is beyond difficult. It feels like an ever ending fight.

I wouldn't be able to cope as well as I do now if it wasn't for the support people have shown me along the way.

I wanna say thank you to everyone who is there for an ear when I need one, a thank you to all of the support groups I attend and most of all a massive thank you to my family.

Donna, Miley and Phoenix for really helping me on my way. I know it hasn't been easy for you either but I'm so glad you've been supporting me through my bad days, I wouldn't get through them without you.

I love you.

Robert Gillett